M-ATVs

BY DENNY VON FINN

EPIC

BELLWETHER MEDIA · MINNEAPOLIS, MN

EPIC BOOKS are no ordinary books. They burst with intense action, high-speed heroics, and shadows of the unknown. Are you ready for an Epic adventure?

This edition first published in 2014 by Bellwether Media, Inc.

No part of this publication may be reproduced in whole or in part without written permission of the publisher. For information regarding permission, write to Bellwether Media, Inc., Attention: Permissions Department, 5357 Penn Avenue South, Minneapolis, MN 55419.

Library of Congress Cataloging-in-Publication Data

Von Finn, Denny.
  M-ATVs / by Denny Von Finn.
     pages cm. – (Epic: military vehicles)
  Includes bibliographical references and index.
  Summary: "Engaging images accompany information about M-ATVs. The combination of high-interest subject matter and light text is intended for students in grades 2 through 7"–Provided by publisher.
  Audience: Ages 6-12.
  ISBN 978-1-60014-943-6 (hbk. : alk. paper)
  1. Armored vehicles, Military–Juvenile literature. I. Title.
  UG446.5.V62 2013
  623.74'75–dc23
                                                                    2013004895

Printed in the United States of America, North Mankato, MN.

The photographs in this book are reproduced through the courtesy of the United States Department of Defense. A special thanks to the following for additional photos: Stocktrek Images/ Getty Images, p. 7; Bob Strong/ Reuters/ Newscom, p. 12; Ed Darack/ Science Faction/ SuperStock, pp. 18-19, 20.

TABLE OF CONTENTS

M-ATVs

An M-ATV rumbles in the morning air. Inside are five Marines. They are on patrol.

The M-ATV rolls over rocks and sand. Shots ring out. One of the tires is hit! The mighty M-ATV keeps going.

M-ATV Fact

An M-ATV can drive more than 30 miles (48 kilometers) after its tires have been shot.

GUNNER

USMC-651956

The M-ATV's **gunner** returns fire. The crew radios for help from aircraft. Then they head back to base.

WEAPONS AND FEATURES

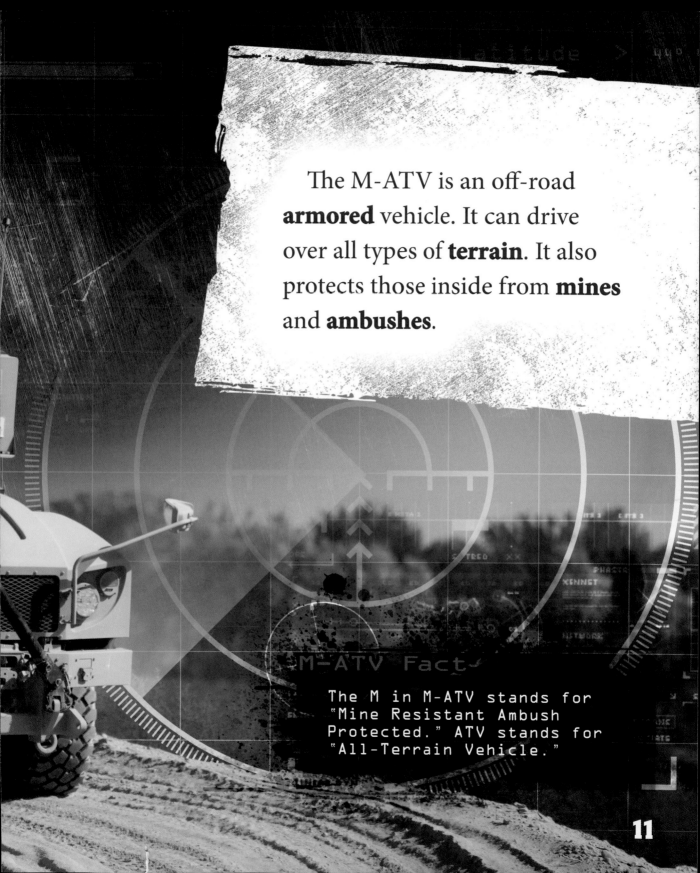

The M-ATV is an off-road **armored** vehicle. It can drive over all types of **terrain**. It also protects those inside from **mines** and **ambushes**.

M-ATV Fact

The M in M-ATV stands for "Mine Resistant Ambush Protected." ATV stands for "All-Terrain Vehicle."

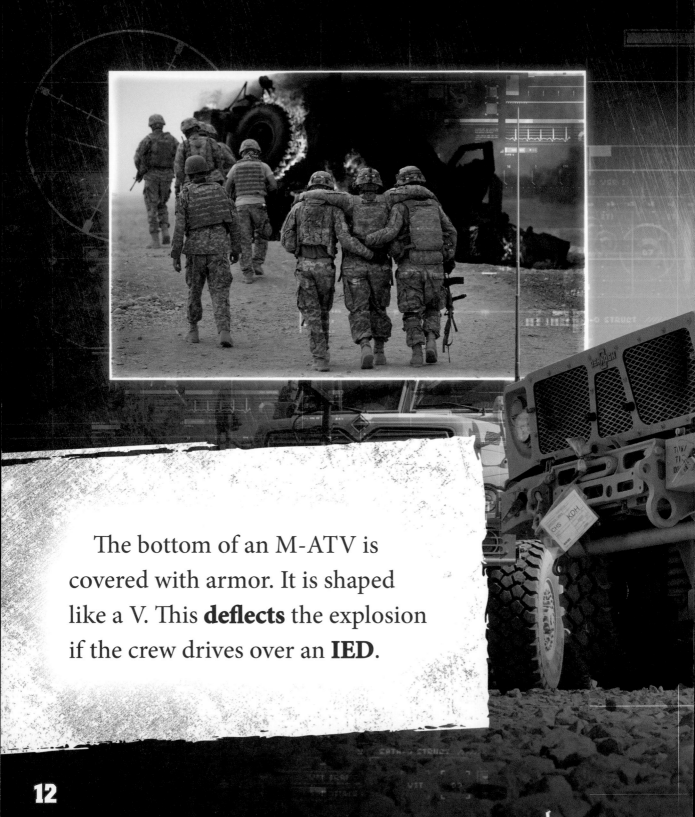

The bottom of an M-ATV is covered with armor. It is shaped like a V. This **deflects** the explosion if the crew drives over an **IED**.

M-ATV Fact

The M-ATV has a tough engine. It can run a short distance after taking a bullet.

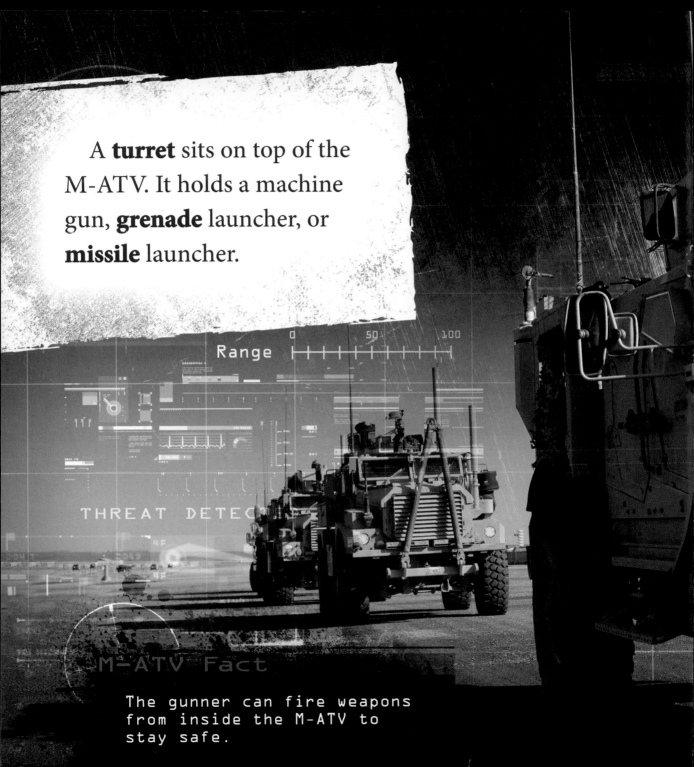

A **turret** sits on top of the M-ATV. It holds a machine gun, **grenade** launcher, or **missile** launcher.

Range

THREAT DETEC

M-ATV Fact

The gunner can fire weapons from inside the M-ATV to stay safe.

TURRET

15

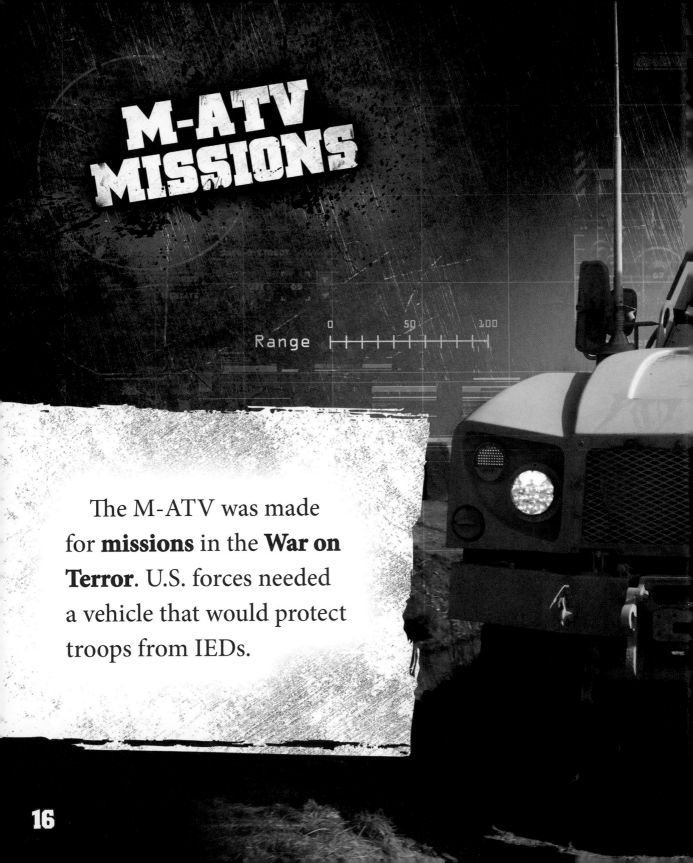

M-ATV MISSIONS

The M-ATV was made for **missions** in the **War on Terror**. U.S. forces needed a vehicle that would protect troops from IEDs.

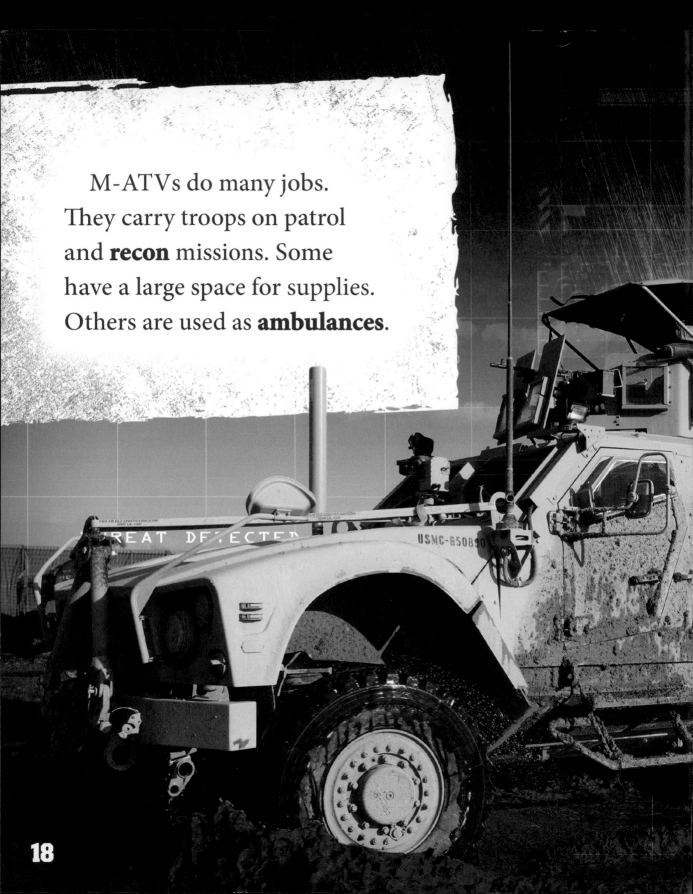

M-ATVs do many jobs. They carry troops on patrol and **recon** missions. Some have a large space for supplies. Others are used as **ambulances**.

M-ATV AMBULANCE

M-ATVs have proven their strength in battle. They will continue to serve long after the war is won!

VEHICLE BREAKDOWN: M-ATV

Used By:	U.S. Air Force
	U.S. Army
	U.S. Marine Corps
	U.S. Navy
Entered Service:	2009
Length:	20 feet, 6 inches (6.3 meters)
Height:	8 feet, 2 inches (2.5 meters)
Vehicle Weight:	25,000 pounds (11,340 kilograms)
Top Speed:	65 miles (105 kilometers) per hour
Range:	320 miles (515 kilometers)
Crew:	5
Weapons:	machine gun, grenade launcher, or missile launcher
Primary Missions:	patrol, recon, troop and cargo transport

GLOSSARY

ambulances—vehicles that bring injured people to hospitals

ambushes—surprise attacks

armored—covered in thick plates called armor; armor protects the M-ATV crew from explosives.

deflects—causes something to scatter

grenade—a small explosive that is either thrown by hand or launched with a special weapon

gunner—the M-ATV crew member who searches for targets and fires the vehicle's weapons

IED—a homemade but very deadly bomb; IED stands for "improvised explosive device."

mines—explosives that are hidden beneath the ground so they explode when vehicles drive over them

missile—an explosive that is guided to its target

missions—military tasks

recon—a type of mission that involves gathering information about the enemy

terrain—a stretch of land

turret—a platform that holds weapons and can turn in any direction

War on Terror—a war led by the United States to stop organized groups from performing acts of violence; the War on Terror began in 2001.

TO LEARN MORE

At the Library

Hamilton, John. *Strykers*. Edina, Minn.: ABDO Pub. Co., 2012.

Jackson, Kay. *Armored Vehicles In Action*. New York, N.Y.: PowerKids Press, 2009.

Von Finn, Denny. *Humvees*. Minneapolis, Minn.: Bellwether Media, 2013.

On the Web

Learning more about M-ATVs
is as easy as 1, 2, 3.

1. Go to www.factsurfer.com.

2. Enter "M-ATVs" into the search box.

3. Click the "Surf" button and you will see a list
of related Web sites.

With factsurfer.com, finding more information
is just a click away.

INDEX